Contents

Chapter 1

Sam Joins the Confederate Army

Clark County, Kentucky
August 15, 1861

Young Sam Jones lived in
north central Kentucky. His
family owned a 300-acre
corn farm. They also had
some livestock. They had a
few cows, a few hogs, and
about a dozen chickens.

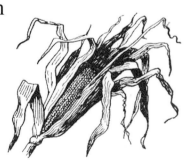

Brothers at War

by L. L. Owens

Perfection Learning®

Cover Design: Alan D. Stanley
Inside Illustration: Greg Hargreaves

About the Author

Lisa L. Owens grew up in the Midwest. She studied English and journalism at the University of Iowa. Currently, she works as an editor and freelance writer in Seattle.

Other Civil War books by Ms. Owens include *Abraham Lincoln: A Great American Life, America's Civil War,* and *The Code of the Drum.*

When his parents died, Sam took over the farm. His older brother, Ned,  moved to Lexington to live with an uncle. Their mother's sister, Lila, moved in with Sam. She ran the household.

One morning, Sam was hard at work. Nate was working in the next field.

Nate and his wife, Effie, were slaves. They'd lived with Sam's family ever since Sam could remember.

"Nate!" Sam called out. "It's getting hot. I think it's time for a break."

"Okay!" Nate agreed.

The men headed to the farmhouse. Effie waved at them from the porch. She was snapping the green beans they would eat for dinner.

"Come sit down," Effie said. "I'll fetch you some nice cool water. I just brought in a fresh batch from the well."

Lila came outside when she heard Sam. She held a piece of paper in her hand.

She said, "This is a letter from your brother. Would you like to read it?"

Sam wanted to. He missed Ned. They had always been best friends. But that was before the Civil War had started. He said, "No thank you, Aunt Lila."

"Oh, Sam," she said. "Are you still angry with him? I don't like it when you boys fight."

"He's the one who left the farm. Not me," Sam answered.

Nate got up and walked inside. "I'll go see what's keeping Effie," he said. He knew that Sam and Lila were about to discuss the war. And he didn't always like what they said.

Lila said, "Now, Sam. Ned has a right to his opinion. Same as you."

"I suppose," Sam said. "But the last time he visited, he called me crazy. Just for wanting to fight for the South. And I'll never understand why he wants to fight for the North. The South is his home!"

"Well, people aren't just fighting according to where they're from. They're fighting for what they believe in. Ned believes in the North's cause," Lila said.

Lila paused. Then she said, "There's something you should know, Sam."

"What is it?" he asked.

"Ned has already joined the army. He'll be fighting for the **Union** by next week."

The **Union** was the United States. It was also called the North. Union soldiers were often called Yankees.

Sam was surprised. He hadn't really thought that Ned would do it.

"Come now," Lila said, hugging him. "Why don't you read Ned's letter? He asks about you."

But Sam was stubborn. He said, "No. I don't want to hear anything that **traitor** has to say."

Sam hurried off the porch. He called over his shoulder, "Please tell Nate that I went back to the fields. Have him spend the rest of the morning patching the hole in the roof. It smells like rain."

A **traitor** is someone who goes against what is expected.

Sam had been in the fields for about three hours. He noticed a gray blur in the distance. It was a group of men. They were all on horseback. They were headed straight for the farm.

Soon they rode up and stopped near the field where Sam was working. "Hello!" a young man shouted. "I'm Bo Granger. Is this the Jones place?"

"It sure is. I'm Sam Jones," Sam replied. "What can I do for you fellas?" Sam could tell that the men were **Confederate** soldiers.

The **Confederacy** was the government of the South. Confederate soldiers were often called Rebels and Johnny Rebs.

"Mr. Sampson at the Winchester general store told us we'd find you here," Bo said. "We need Kentucky men to join our forces. The battle lines are moving this way."

Sam had planned to join up. But he'd wanted to bring in the crops first.

"I thought I'd join up in about six weeks or so," Sam said.

"That'll be too late," Bo said. "We need you now."

Sam thought for a moment. Then he said, "Okay. But let me go back to the house. I need to pack a few things."

"No need to pack anything," Bo said. "The army will give you some gear. Besides, we're in a hurry to get back. Our unit is moving out tonight."

"May I at least say good-bye to my aunt?" Sam asked. "She'll worry if I don't."

"Okay," Bo agreed. "Hop on the back of my horse. I'll run you over to see her."

The horse thundered across the field. Lila looked up from picking goldenrods. She turned pale when she noticed the soldier. Somehow, she knew that Sam was about to say good-bye.

Bo stopped his horse. Sam climbed down.

"This is Bo Granger, Aunt Lila," Sam said.

"Hello, Mr. Granger," she said. "It's a pleasure to meet you."

"Hello, ma'am," Bo replied.

Lila asked, "May I offer you something to eat?"

"No, thank you, ma'am."

Sam said, "He can't stay. And neither can I. He's taking me back to his army unit. Looks like it's time for me to join the war."

"Well," Lila sighed. "We knew it would happen sooner or later."

She felt scared. Now both of her nephews would be fighting in dangerous battles. And they'd be on different sides of the war! She prayed that they would never have to fight each other.

"Will you manage things for me here, Aunt Lila?" Sam asked.

"Of course," she said. "I can hire someone to help bring in the crops. Don't worry."

Sam hugged Lila hard. Softly he said, "Take care of yourself. Say good-bye to Nate and Effie for me."

"I will," Lila said. "Try to stay safe. And be sure to write."

Sam hopped back onto the horse. He and Bo joined the rest of the soldiers and headed for their camp.

Lila watched them ride away. Soon they looked like a tiny moving speck. Then they disappeared where the sky met the hillside.

Chapter 2

Ned Joins the Union Army

Lexington, Kentucky
August 15, 1861

Ned Jones stared out the kitchen window. He thought about his family. He missed them. And he missed the farm.

He missed Sam the most. He felt terrible about the fight they'd had.

Ned liked living with Uncle William, though. William built furniture. He was teaching Ned the trade.

William also helped slaves escape to the North. His home was a **station** on a secret path. It led to the freedom of the North. That path was called the Underground Railroad.

A **station** was a safe house, barn, or shelter on the Underground Railroad. The Underground Railroad was a system of stations and people who helped slaves escape from the South.

Sometimes escaped slaves spent the night in William's hidden attic. Sometimes William hid slaves in his wagon. Then he'd drive them to the next station.

Slaves on the run usually traveled at night. It was safer that way. Fewer people were likely to see them.

Some slave owners hired people to find their slaves. They also offered rewards to anyone who spotted or caught the runaways.

If caught, slaves were forced to go back to their owners. Most were then beaten. Even William was in danger for helping the slaves.

At dusk each evening, William tied back a curtain in an upstairs window. That was his signal to escaping slaves. It meant that it was safe to knock on his door. It was safe to ask for help.

When the curtain was down, people knew not to knock. It meant that William had guests. Or someone might be watching.

Ned had moved in with William the year before. He hadn't heard of the Underground Railroad.

William had explained everything shortly after Ned arrived. He'd said, "I feel it is my duty to help people to freedom. That's why I'm part of the system. You'll have to help if you live in this house. You'll also have to keep everything we do a secret. Can I count on you?"

"You sure can, Uncle William," Ned replied.

Ned was against slavery too. He was happy and proud to help.

Ned recalled a talk he'd had with his uncle years earlier. Ned must have been about 11 years old. It was the first time he'd really thought about whether slavery was right or wrong.

William said—
"You see, Ned. I believe that no man has a right to own another."

"But our family owns Nate and Effie," Ned said. "Do you think that's wrong?"

"Yes, I do, son," William replied. "Your folks treat them well. Like part of the family. But that doesn't make it fair."

"Why not?" Ned asked. "We love Nate and Effie. And they seem happy here."

"Nate and Effie love you too. I'm sure they are happy in many ways. But you have to understand where they came from."

William continued. "Your dad bought them from Mr. Jeffreys. He's a cruel plantation owner. He works his slaves to the bone. Most work in his tobacco fields.

"He's been known to beat—and even kill—his slaves. They live in fear. And in poverty," William said. "Meanwhile, Mr. Jeffreys lives like a king. He has that beautiful house. It was built from the  profits of years of slave labor.

"So it is true," William went on. "Nate and Effie are better off than they used to be. Yet they are still slaves. They have no choices open to them. They have to work for your dad. Their lives are in his hands."

"Isn't working for us just like working at any other job?" Ned asked. "Tom at the Sampsons' store has to do whatever Mr. Sampson says. Right? That's how he gets paid.

"Nate and Effie work for our family," Ned continued. "And they do what Dad says. But Dad gives them food and a place to live instead of money."

William nodded. "But think about it, Ned. Nate and Effie aren't free to leave if they want to. They're black. Around here that means that they can't even look for other work."

He continued. "Tom can. He's white. He can choose what he wants to do. Same goes for your dad. If he wanted to stop farming, he could get another job.

"Nate and Effie aren't that lucky," William said. "Freedom's a precious thing. And they just don't have it."

Ned gave the matter some thought. Then he talked to Nate.

"Do you and Effie ever think about leaving us?" Ned asked him.

"Of course not," Nate replied. "Where would we go?"

Ned said, "You could go north to Pennsylvania. Or even Canada. You and Effie could find work up there. I'm sure of it."

"What's got into you, child?" Nate asked. "You know we can't leave your folks."

"Why not?" Ned asked.

"We belong to them," Nate answered. "They have the legal papers to prove it."

"I'll bet they'd let you go if you really wanted to," said Ned.

"Ned . . ." Nate began. He shook his head. "It's not that simple. Even if your folks said we could leave, we wouldn't make it out of the county. Folks around here wouldn't let us. We'd be arrested. Or killed. Or put up for auction."

Nate looked right at Ned. "Who knows where we'd end up then? Someone as horrible as Mr. Jeffreys could buy us. Why, Effie and I could even be sold to different masters. I'd rather stay right here forever than take those kinds of chances."

Ned struggled to understand. "Don't you want to be free?" he asked.

Nate got very quiet. Finally, he replied solemnly, "I learned a long time ago not to waste time dreaming. Not about something that's never going to happen. It hurts too much."

Nate paused. Then he added, "Now— you'd better scoot. I've got work to do."

Ned never forgot the sadness he saw in Nate's eyes that day.

During his time with William, Ned helped many slaves. He often thought about Nate and Effie. He vowed to someday help them too.

Maybe I can if the North wins the war, he thought.

William walked into the kitchen. "What are you thinking about, Ned?"

"Home. And the war," Ned replied. "Do you think I did the right thing? Joining the Union army, I mean?"

"You know what *I* think," William said. "The most important thing, though, is what *you* think."

"I think that keeping the nation together is worth fighting for," said Ned. "The U.S. will crumble if it splits in two. I also agree with President Lincoln. He said, 'Government cannot endure permanently half slave, half free.' Plus,  I think that slavery is plain wrong."

William chuckled. "Seems that you know your own mind after all. I'm proud of you."

"I wish Sam could be proud of me," Ned said. "He may never forgive me for joining the Union army."

"You boys are brothers," said William. "You can forgive each other anything. Maybe it won't happen till after the war. But it will happen. You'll see."

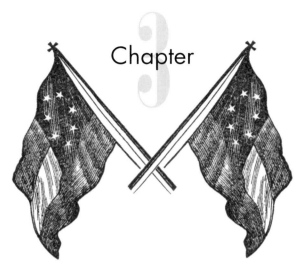

Chapter 3

Sam's War

Barbourville, Kentucky
September 19, 1861

Sam awoke from a quick nap. It was about 3 A.M. His unit planned to attack Camp Andrew Johnson at daylight. It would be a long day.

He gathered up his bedroll. Then he pulled on his heavy gray jacket over his cotton shirt and wool vest.

Sam had slept in his gray trousers and ankle-high boots. All the soldiers did. They had to be ready to move or fight anytime— even as they slept!

Sam had been a soldier for more than a month. Being a soldier was hard work. He was always tired and sore. His unit moved around a lot. They tried to stay one step ahead of the Union.

Sam joined some other men outside his tent. For breakfast, they made coffee in a kettle over the fire. It tasted awful. But the soldiers drank it. It helped wash down the hard, stale corn bread they ate every day.

Colonel Joel Battle came out of his tent. "We start marching in half an hour," he said.

Sam was nervous. This would be his first battle. He knew it would be hard to see people die. And it scared him to know that he could die too.

He thought of Ned. "I hope he's not there today," he said to himself. He'd stopped being angry at Ned long ago. Out here, their differences didn't seem to matter.

The troops marched out on schedule. They headed toward the Union training camp.

Along the way, they sang a Confederate song. It was called "The Bonnie Blue Flag."

We are a band of brothers
And native to the soil,
Fighting for the property
We gained by honest toil;
And when our
    rights were
    threatened,
The cry rose
    near and far—
"Hurrah for
    the Bonnie
    Blue Flag
That bears a
    single star!"

Chorus: Hurrah! Hurrah!
For Southern rights, hurrah!
Hurrah for the Bonnie Blue Flag
That bears a single star.

As long as the Union
Was faithful to her trust,
Like friends and
   like brothers
Both kind were
   we and just;
But now, when
   Northern treachery
Attempts our rights to mar,
We hoist on high the Bonnie Blue Flag
That bears a single star.

Chorus

Ye men of valor, gather round
The banner of the right;
Texas and fair Louisiana
Join us in the fight.
Davis, our loved president,
And Stephens statesmen are;
Now rally round the Bonnie Blue Flag
That bears a single star.

Chorus

Then here's to our Confederacy,
Strong are we and brave;
Like patriots of old we'll fight
Our heritage to save.
And rather than submit to shame,
To die we would prefer;
So cheer for the Bonnie Blue Flag
That bears a single star.

Soon the men reached the camp. They stormed in. But they were surprised. Most of the recruits had been moved! Colonel Battle's troops outnumbered the Union's 800 to 300!

The Confederates destroyed the camp as they fought. They also stole arms and other supplies.

The Union troops fought back as hard as they could. "Kill the Rebels!" ordered the Union's Captain Isaac Black.

The two sides shot at each other. Some men fought with bayonets. Sam had never seen so much blood.

The Union fired a cannon. Sam was nearby. The deafening sound hurt his ears. He got distracted. He tripped over a wounded man.

Sam saw a Yankee soldier take aim—right at him! He darted to the side. He took cover behind a barrel. The enemy bullet hit someone else in Sam's unit.

Sam didn't know what to feel. He had saved himself. But it had cost someone else his life. Sam felt sick to his stomach.

Then he saw Bo across the road. A Union soldier was about to attack him from behind. Sam knew what he had to do. He aimed and fired. He hit his mark—he saved Bo!

Without warning, Sam's right leg twisted out from under him. He landed on his back. He was dazed. But he didn't feel any pain.

Bo ran to Sam's side. He yelled to the field surgeon.

"Sam's been hit in the knee! Over here! Quick!"

That was the last thing that Sam remembered from the battle. He woke up in the hospital two days later. His right leg had been amputated. He was shocked and sad when he found out. And now he felt the pain. But he was glad to be alive.

He sent word to Aunt Lila. She'd need to know that he was coming home.

Sam's war was over.

Chapter 4

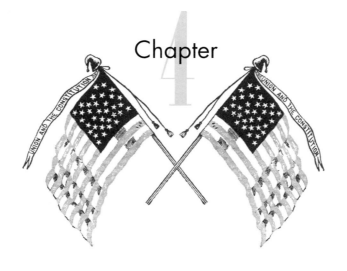

Ned's War

Wildcat Mountain, Kentucky
October 21, 1861

Ned scratched his shoulder. But he couldn't get rid of the itch. It was too hard to scratch through his heavy Union uniform.

He wore a dark blue flannel coat, white flannel shirt, blue wool trousers, wool socks, and leather boots. Ned was in the infantry. So he had sky-blue stripes running down the outer seam of his uniform.

Ned's unit was moving on that day. He checked his gear. He wanted to make sure he had everything.

A soldier's gear included
- a rifle
- a cartridge box
- a bayonet
- a cap box
- a canvas haversack, or bag, with some food and eating utensils in it
- a tin canteen and cup
- a bar of soap
- a towel
- a jackknife
- a shaving kit

Walter and Donald stopped by the tent Ned shared with James. "Are you guys ready?" Walter asked.

"Just about," Ned replied. He finished packing and storing his gear. His friends kept him company.

Half an hour later, Brigadier General Albin Schoepf issued the marching orders.

As they marched, Ned called out, "Let's sing that song Donald taught us last night."

The men launched into a Union song. It was called "Reply to 'The Bonnie Blue Flag.'"

We're fighting
   for our Union,
We're fighting
   for our trust,
We're fighting for that
   happy land
Where sleeps our
   fathers' dust.
It cannot be [divided],
Though it cost us
   bloody wars,
We never can give up the land
Where floats the stripes and stars.

   Chorus: Hurrah, Hurrah,
   For equal rights, hurrah,
   Hurrah for the good old flag
   That bears the stripes and stars.

We trusted you as brothers,
Until you drew the sword,
With [cruel] hands at Sumter

You cut the silver cord.
So now you hear the bugles,
We come the sons of Mars,
To rally round the brave old flag
That bears the stripes and stars.

Chorus

We do not want your cotton,
We do not want your slaves,
But rather than divide the land,
We'll fill your Southern graves.
With Lincoln for our chieftain,
We wear our country's stars,
And rally round the
    brave old flag
That bears the stripes
    and stars.

Chorus

And when this war is over,
We'll each resume our home,
And treat you still as brothers,
Wherever you may roam.
We'll pledge the hand of friendship,
And think no more of war,
But dwell in peace beneath the flag
That bears the stripes and stars.

Suddenly, General Schoepf cried, "Rebels straight ahead! Battle stance, men!"

The men threw down their packs and took up their weapons. An unexpected battle had begun. It would last all day.

The air was thick with smoke. Ned blinked hard as he ran across the field. He looked for his friends. He saw Walter and Donald. They were safe. But where was James?

"James!" he shouted. "Where are you? James! Can you hear me?"

Ned's words were lost in the chaos. Men called out for help. Some screamed with pain. Many sobbed with fear. Others lay still. They were waiting to die.

The Confederates were still shooting. Bullets whizzed past Ned's ears.

Ned saw James. The two nearly ran into each other.

"James! I'm so glad that you're okay," said Ned.

"Same to you," said James. "I've been looking for you for hours. Have you seen Walter and Donald?"

"Yes," Ned replied. He spotted them again. "Here they come!"

Ned and James hurried to meet their friends. "We're all in this together," said James.

Just then a cannon roared. Ned and James watched in horror as Walter and Donald were hit!

"No!" Ned and James both cried. They tried to run to their friends. But an officer ordered them to turn around.

"Leave them!" he cried. "You can't help them now!"

Ned and James followed orders. And they helped their troops force the Confederates to retreat.

It was a Union victory. But Ned and James couldn't cheer with the others. They were too upset at losing their good friends.

Later, the men warmed themselves in front of a campfire. Ned thought about Sam. "I wonder where he is? I wonder if he was there today?"

"I hate the Rebels," James said. "I wish we could have killed those two who fired the cannon."

"I don't," Ned said.

"They killed Walter and Donald," protested James.

"I know," answered Ned, "but we don't know *who* they were."

James glared at Ned. "Sure we do. They're Johnny Rebs."

"We didn't see their faces," Ned said. His voice got louder. "So, like I said, we *don't* know *who* they were!"

"It doesn't matter who they were—" James said.

"It does to me, James!" shouted Ned.

James left Ned alone for a few minutes. Then he asked quietly, "What's the matter?"

"I have no idea where my brother is fighting. So I'm always afraid that the next Rebel we kill will be him."

"I'm sorry," James said. "I wasn't thinking about your brother. That must be hard for you."

"It sure is," Ned said. "Guess I'm thinking about him even more since seeing all those men die today."

He continued. "I'll be able to take a few days of leave this winter. I can visit the farm. Maybe Aunt Lila has heard from Sam."

Chapter 5

The Brothers Come Face-to-Face

Ned neared the farm. His heart swelled. He'd missed the place very much. He could hardly wait to see Lila, Nate, and Effie.

It was past dark when he tied up his horse outside. He figured everyone had been in bed for hours. He crept inside, hoping not to wake anyone. But someone was sitting in front of the fire.

Slowly, Sam turned and faced his brother.

"Sam!" Ned gasped. "You're home too!" He rushed to Sam's side. As he reached out to hug him, he knocked over something propped against Sam's chair.

"I'm sorry, Sam," Ned said. "Let me pick those up." He bent down. "What are these?"

Then Ned's eyes adjusted to the dim light. He realized that he was holding a pair of crutches. To Sam, he said, "You've been hurt."

"Yes," Sam replied. "I lost my leg."

"Oh, Sam, no!" Ned exclaimed.

The brothers sat up the rest of the night. They shared battle stories.

Ned tried to comfort Sam. But Sam wouldn't hear of it.

"People get hurt at war," he said. "I knew that when I joined up. I'm just lucky that I survived. Lots of men don't."

"You're right about that," said Ned. "Death is all around. I've lost some friends. I couldn't bear to lose a brother too."

"Does that mean you're not mad at me anymore?" Sam teased.

Ned laughed. "That depends. Are you still mad at me?"

Sam offered his hand for a handshake. Ned happily took it in his own.

"Listen, Sam. I think it's time you knew something," Ned said.

"Go ahead," Sam said.

"I worked closely with Uncle William before I joined the army."

"I know that," said Sam. "He was teaching you how to build furniture."

"Yes, but there's more to it than that."

Ned told Sam about working for the Underground Railroad. He trusted his brother. He knew that Sam would never tell anyone—even if he didn't agree.

"Why are you telling me all this?" asked Sam.

"Because I'd like to help Nate and Effie move north," Ned said. "I'd need your help, though. You'd need to sign some freedom papers and see that they get out of here safely."

"Are you kidding?" asked Sam. "Nate and Effie don't want to go anywhere."

"How do you know? Have you ever asked them?"

"I don't need to," said Sam. "They should stay here. They're part of the family."

"Don't you see, Sam? They're *not* family. We can't say that they are *and* still claim to own them."

44

"Nate and Effie are slaves. Human beings with no rights. A man and his wife with no freedom. Deep down, I think you know that."

"*I* still think of them as family," Sam said firmly. His stubborn streak was showing.

"Then why won't you fight for them?" Ned asked.

"What are you talking about?" Sam asked.

"You stood right here one day and told me that I should fight for the South. Just because I live in it. That it was more important than fighting for the country. Just like fighting for your town was more important than fighting for the South. And fighting for your home was more important than fighting for your town. And fighting for your family was more important than fighting for *anything*."

Sam was silent for a moment. Then he said, "Haven't you forgotten something?"

"What?" Ned asked.

Sam pointed to his legs. "I can't fight at all."

"I'm not talking about fighting with guns. Or even with fists," Ned replied. "I'm talking about fighting with love and support. And help."

Ned went on. "If you truly think of Nate and Effie as family, you'll fight for them. You'll offer them their freedom. And you'll help make it happen."

Sam Makes a Decision

Sam made his way to the barn. He had become skilled at getting around on his crutches.

Sam wanted to see his horse. He couldn't ride her anymore. But he could still talk to her. Besides, stroking her soft nose always made him feel better.

It had been several weeks since Ned's short visit. Since then, Sam had done a lot of thinking. That was one of the things he liked best about his brother. Ned always made him think.

Sam saw his horse, Lucy, and smiled. "Hello, girl," he said. "You look like you could use a brushing."

Then he noticed Nate. Nate was mending one of the saddles.

"Good morning, Nate," Sam said.

"Mornin'," Nate replied. "Looks like you're doing fine with those crutches."

"It does get easier. Have you seen the brush?" Sam asked.

"It's right behind you. Would you like me to brush Lucy?"

"I can do it, Nate."

"Are you sure?" Nate asked.

Sam had already moved toward the brush. Nate watched as Sam bent down on his good leg.

Sam grabbed the brush and put it under his chin. Then he tried to raise himself using his crutches. As one crutch slipped out of Sam's grasp, Nate dashed over and caught him.

"Thanks, Nate," Sam said. "You should have let me fall. I need to learn my limits."

Nate smiled, "I've been catching you since you first stood up. I don't reckon I could ever stand by and watch you fall."

Nate returned to the saddle. Sam leaned against the stall. He talked as Nate worked.

"You know," he said, "they told me that living with just one leg would be hard. I knew there'd be things I couldn't do. Like working the fields and riding. But I never thought about all the little things. Like hiking up a rocky trail. Dancing. Or just holding something in my hands while I walk."

Nate nodded.

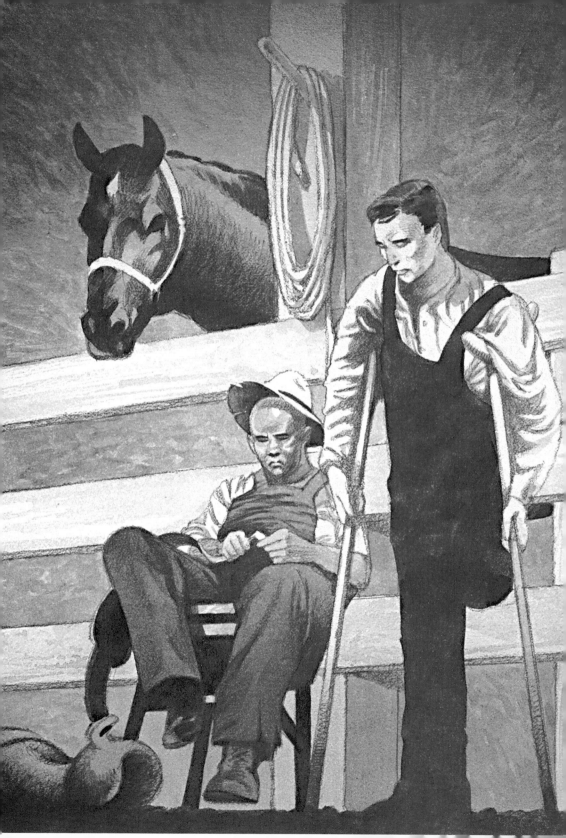

Sam went on. "I guess I didn't realize how important the everyday things are in life. It's hard when you lose your freedom."

Nate looked up for a split second. Then his gaze went right back down at the saddle.

Sam noticed the look. He wondered what he'd said. Then it hit him. *It's hard when you lose your freedom.*

That evening, Sam wrote to Ned. He told him about Nate and the barn and how he'd talked about freedom.

I stood there complaining about my loss of freedom. Right in front of Nate, who's never even *tasted* freedom. And Nate didn't call me on it. Why? Because he's a slave! A slave would never dare scold his master for dwelling on missing freedom. Not even when he helped raise his master. Not even when the slave is Nate and the master is *me*.

Sam put down his pen. He thought about how loyal Nate and Effie were to the family. And he knew what he had to do.

Chapter 7

The Drive to Freedom

"I'll be back soon, Aunt Lila!" Sam called from the wagon.

"See that you are, Sam," she replied. "And give my regards to your Uncle William."

"I will," he promised.

Sam turned to Nate and Effie. They both had happy tears in their eyes.

Nate said, "I never thought I'd see this day."

"I know," Sam said. "I'm sorry that it took me so long to make it happen."

"No use talking like that," Effie said. "What's done is done. You've been good to us. And now you've given us our freedom. It says so. Right here." She tapped the papers that  Sam had signed. "We're grateful to you."

Sam began the drive to Lexington. They would stop at Uncle William's house. From there, William had arranged for Nate and Effie's safe passage to New York.

While driving, Sam listened to Nate and Effie make plans.

"I could get a job as a seamstress," Effie said. "Maybe you could work with horses, Nate."